(6) Knowledge in Islam

A Collection of Quranic Verses and Sayings from the 14 Ma'soomeen

According to ahadith, human beings are in a state of loss, unless they are in one of the following states: (1) learning and understanding, (2) teaching, (3) practicing what they have learned, or (4) preparing to learn or practice. Therefore, it is important for us to constantly seek and attain further knowledge, which includes more than just the systemic school education. Parents should ensure their children are educated holistically and learn all they need to live a successful life both in this world and the next.

يَرْفَعِ اللّهُ الَّذِينَ ءَامَنُوا مِنكُمْ وَ الَّذِينَ أُوتُوا الْعِلْمَ دَرَجَاتٍ

Allah will raise the status of those among you
who have faith and have been given knowledge.

Sūrah al-Mujādilah, Verse 11

One day, Prophet Muhammad (s) entered the masjid and saw two groups of people. The first group was busy praying, while the second group was in the middle of a lively discussion about important issues.

The Prophet (s) then said, "Allah is pleased with what both of these groups are doing, but I will join the second group because Allah sent me to teach people and help them understand things better."

When we learn more about who Allah is, our acts of worship usually become much more special. Our prayers are worth much more when we come to realize more about what is true in the world.

Anecdotes of Pious Men

إِنَّ الْمَلَائِكَةَ لَتَضَعُ أَجْنِحَتَهَا لِطَالِبِ الْعِلْمِ

Prophet Muhammad (s):
Indeed, angels spread out their wings [out of respect]
for the seekers of knowledge.

Biḥār ul-Anwār, Vol. 1, P. 177

وَ الْقَلَمِ وَ مَا يَسْطُرُونَ

By the pen and by what they write.

Sūrah al-Qalam, Verse 1

One day, Imam Hasan (a) gathered a group of young people from his family and told them, "today you are children, but tomorrow you will be leaders; so work hard to learn and understand. If you can't remember what your teacher said in class, take notes so that you can review them whenever you need to."

Biḥār ul-Anwār, Vol.2, P.152

قَيِّدُوا الْعِلْمَ بِالْكِتَابَة

Prophet Muhammad (s):
Save knowledge through note-taking.

History of Shīʿah Ḥadīth, Vol. 1, P. 17

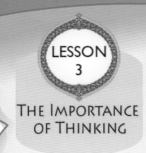

أَفَلَا تَتَفَكَّرُونَ

Will you not think?

Sūrah al-Anʿām, Verse 50

One day, Prophet Muhammad (s) saw a man sitting by himself, deep in thought. So he sat beside him and asked, "What are you thinking about?"

The man said, "Allah says in the Quran that smart people think about the wonders of the world, so I'm thinking about how Allah created everything so perfectly and beautifully!"

The Prophet (s) then said, "SubhaanAllah! Did you know that one hour of thinking is better than a whole year of worship?"

As human beings, we always need to make time to think about things in silence. There are so many important things to figure out in our heads. Our minds should be busy thinking about things like how we've spent our lives, how we plan to become better people, how Allah gave us so many blessings, how best to use our time, and so on.

100 Topics, 500 Stories

فَضْلُ فِكْرٍ وَ تَفَهُّمٍ أَنْجَعُ مِنْ فَضْلِ تَكْرَارٍ وَ دِرَاسَةٍ

Imam Ali (a):
To think about something and try to understand it is more useful than to just read and memorize.

Ghurar al-Ḥikam, Durar al-Kalām, #6564

فَاسْئَلُوا أَهْلَ الذِّكْرِ إِنْ كُنْتُمْ لَا تَعْلَمُونَ

If you don't know something, ask those who
[know] and always remember Allah.

Sūrah al-Anbiyā', Verse 7

Sayyidah Fatimah (a) used to teach Quran to the women of Medina. In one of these gatherings, one woman asked so many questions. Sayyidah Fatimah (a) made sure to answer all of them patiently and with a smile.

After the woman asked her tenth question, she felt embarrassed and said, "I bothered you with so many questions today!" and Sayyidah (a) gently replied, "Ask as many questions as you would like and I will gladly reply. Allah gives thousands of rewards for every answer that I give."

Whenever you have a question - whether it's big or small - don't be shy to ask. Ask the right people — people who know more about the subject you're wondering about. You can also save your questions for later, when you meet with a teacher or scholar.

Biḥār ul-Anwār, Vol. 2, P. 3

اَلسُّؤَالُ نِصْفُ الْعِلْم

Prophet Muhammad (S):
A good question is half of knowledge.

Kanz ul-'Ummāl, #29260

وَ قُل رَّبِّ زِدْنِي عِلْمًا

And say, "My Lord, give me more knowledge."

Sūrah Tāha, Verse 114

Allah once asked Prophet Musa (a), "Who is the most knowledgeable person?"

He replied, "I do not know anyone more knowledgeable than You, O Allah. And You have also given special knowledge to me."

Allah then told him, "yes, O Musa, I am the Most Knowledgeable, and from My servants, al-Khidr (a) is more knowledgeable than you."

After hearing this, Prophet Musa (a) really wanted to meet al-Khidr (a) and learn from him. So, he went in search of him.

When he found al-Khidr (a), he thanked Allah for this blessing. For Prophet Musa (a), it was a very special moment to finally meet him! He thought to himself, *I will try to learn everything I can from al-Khidr.*

At one point, they were walking together along the coast, when they saw a bird filling its beak with water from the ocean and pouring it onto the ground. Al-Khidr (a) asked, "do you know why this bird is doing this?"

Prophet Musa (a) shook his head and listened carefully to what al-Khidr (a) was about to say. "This is Allah's way of showing us that our knowledge compared to His knowledge is like a drop in the gigantic ocean."

Tafsīr Nūr, Vol. 7, P. 399

سَلُوا اللَّهَ عِلْمَاً نَافِعاً

Prophet Muhammad (s):
Ask Allah for useful knowledge.

Nahjul Faṣāḥah, #1743

QUIZ TIME!

1. When entering the masjid, the Prophet (s) saw that one group of people was busy praying and the other was _____.
a. reading Qur'an
b. having a feast
c. in the middle of a beneficial discussion

2. Imam Hasan (a) says that if you cannot remember what your teacher said in class, you should _____.
a. repeat the idea in your head
b. take notes
c. ask a friend

3. According to the Prophet (s), one hour of _____ is better than one year of worshipping.
a. thinking
b. reading Quran
c. playing

4. The Prophet (s) tells us that asking useful questions is half of _____.
a. heaven
b. knowledge
c. rewards

5. Who is the most knowledgeable?
a. Al-Khidr (a)
b. Prophet Muhammad (s)
c. Allah

6. Name two things you learned from this book.

EMAIL YOUR ANSWERS TO QUIZZES@KISAKIDS.ORG, AND WE WILL SEND YOU A CERTIFICATE!